FIVE FINGER PIANO

Fun Songs

T0079312

ISBN 978-1-5400-9493-3

HAL•LEONARD®

Visit Hal Leonard Online at
www.halleonard.com

Contact us:
Hal Leonard
7777 West Bluemound Road
Milwaukee, WI 53213
Email: info@halleonard.com

In Europe, contact:
Hal Leonard Europe Limited
42 Wigmore Street
Marylebone, London, W1U 2RN
Email: info@halleonardeurope.com

In Australia, contact:
Hal Leonard Australia Pty. Ltd.
4 Lentara Court
Cheltenham, Victoria, 3192 Australia
Email: info@halleonard.com.au

CONTENTS

The Ants Go Marching

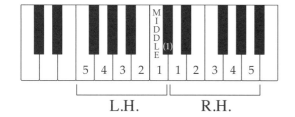

Traditional

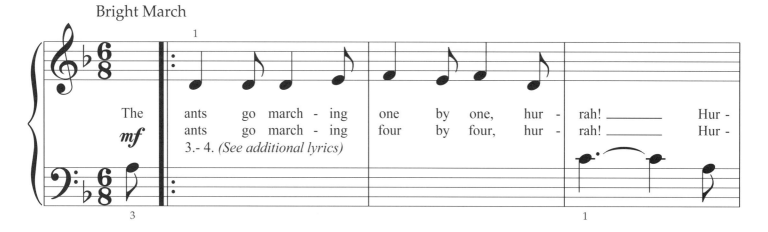

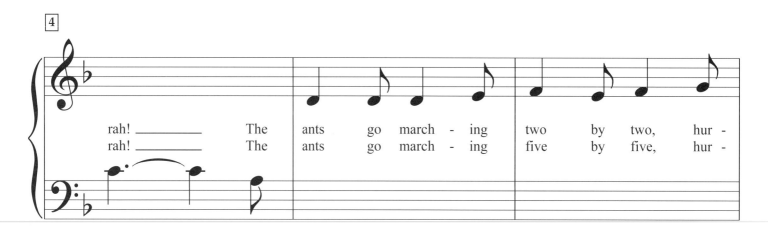

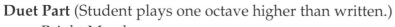

Duet Part (Student plays one octave higher than written.)

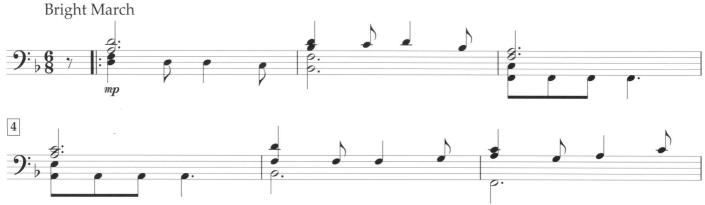

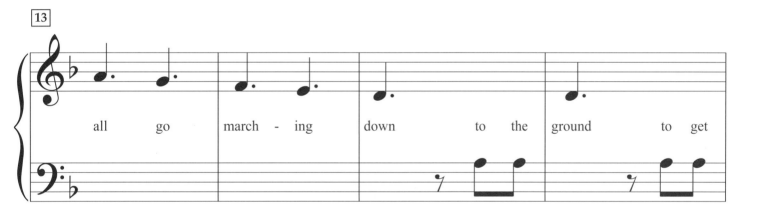

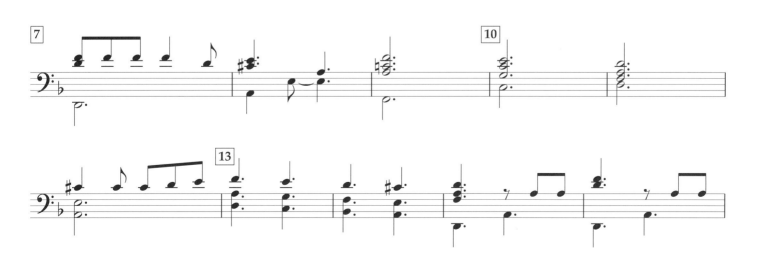

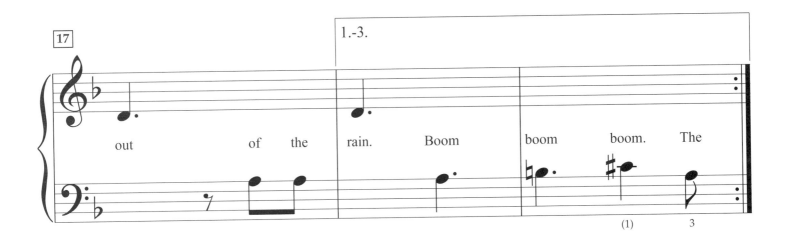

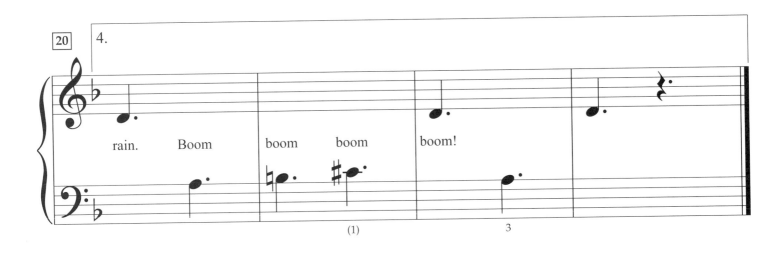

Additional Lyrics

3. The ants go marching seven by seven, hurrah! Hurrah!
   The ants go marching eight by eight, hurrah! Hurrah!
   The ants go marching nine by nine.
   The little one stops to check the time
   And they all go marching down to the ground
   To get out of the rain. Boom boom boom.

4. The ants go marching ten by ten, hurrah! Hurrah!
   The ants go marching ten by ten, hurah! Hurrah!
   The ants go marching ten by ten.
   The little one stops to say "The end!"
   And they all go marching down to the ground
   To get out of the rain. Boom boom boom boom!

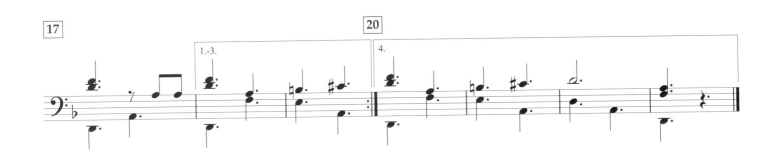

Pop Goes the Weasel

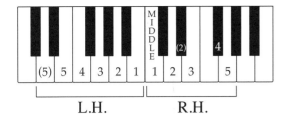

Traditional

Lively

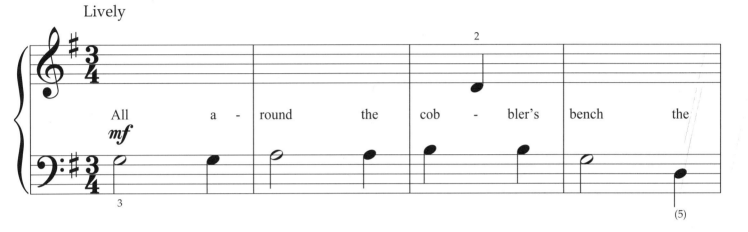

All a - round the cob - bler's bench the

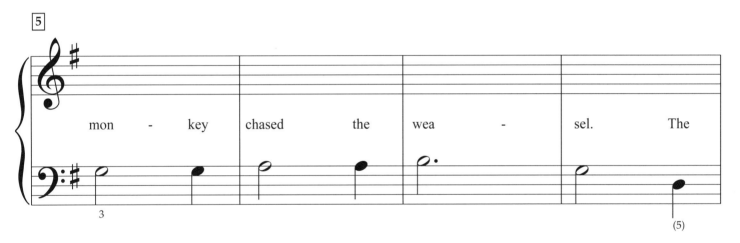

mon - key chased the wea - sel. The

Duet Part (Student plays one octave higher than written.)

Lively

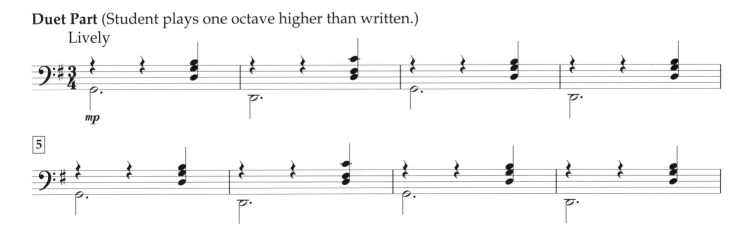

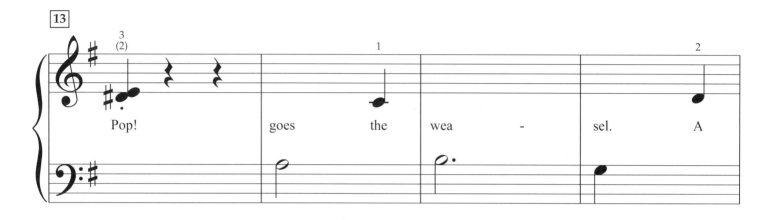

mon - key   thought   'twas   all _____ in   fun.

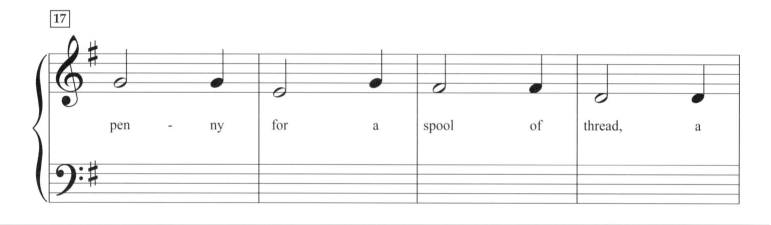

Pop!   goes   the   wea -   sel.   A

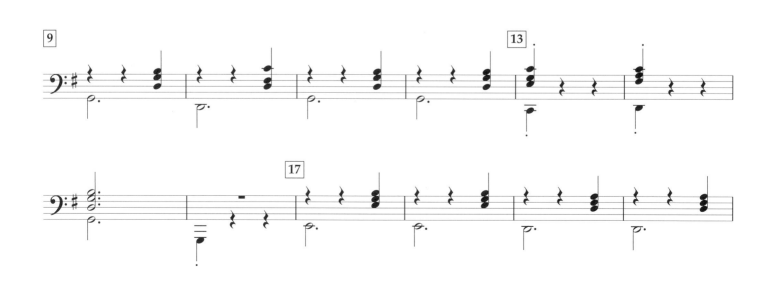

pen - ny   for   a   spool   of   thread,   a

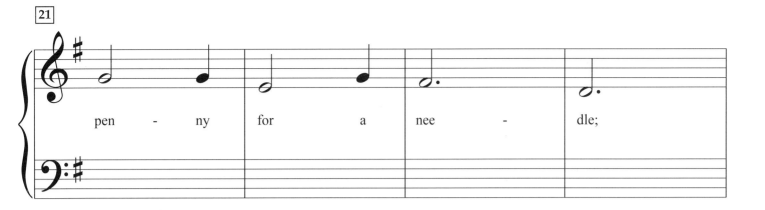

pen - ny   for   a   nee - dle;

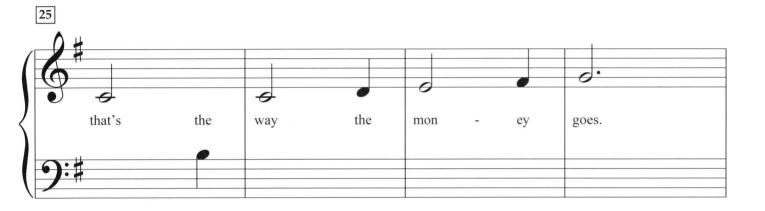

that's   the   way   the   mon - ey   goes.

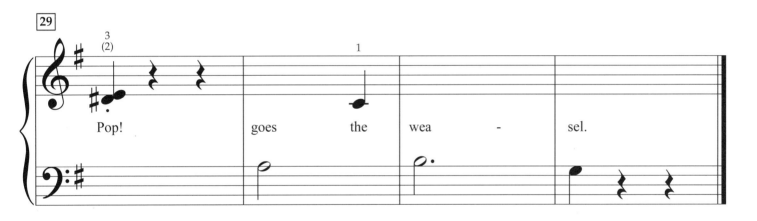

Pop!   goes   the   wea - sel.

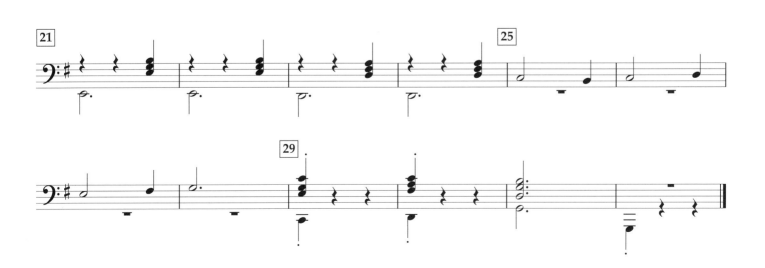

Be Kind to Your Web-Footed Friends

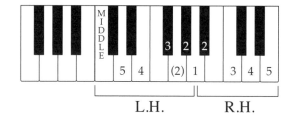

Traditional

Bright March

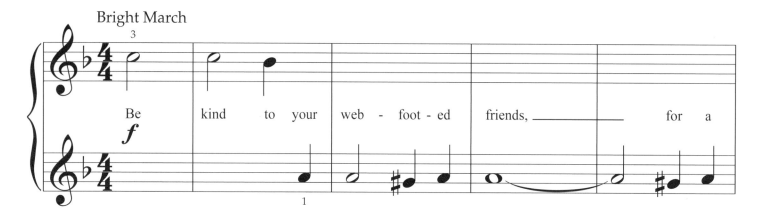

Be kind to your web-foot-ed friends, _____ for a

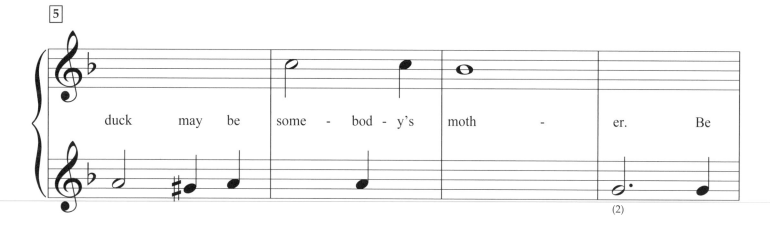

duck may be some-bod-y's moth - er. Be

Duet Part (Student plays one octave higher than written.)
Bright March

Bingo

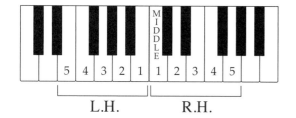

Traditional

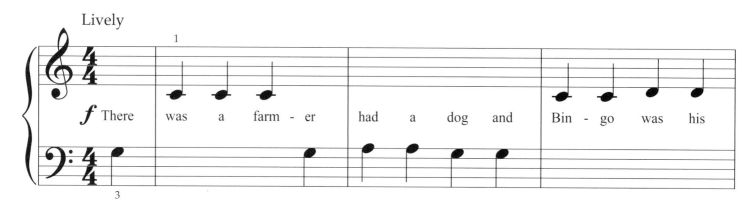

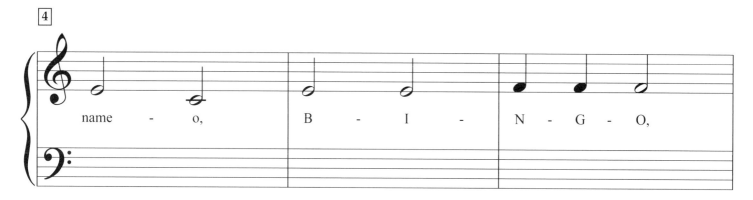

Duet Part (Student plays two octaves higher than written.)

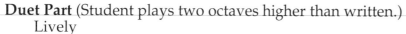

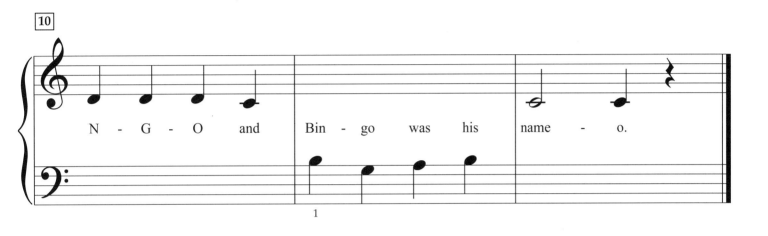

I Know an Old Lady Who Swallowed a Fly

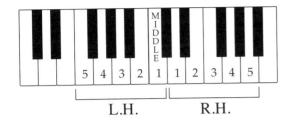

Traditional

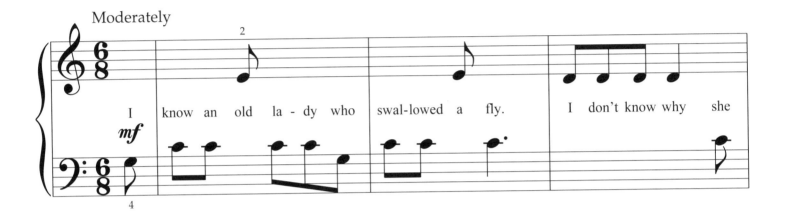

Duet Part (Student plays one octave higher than written.)

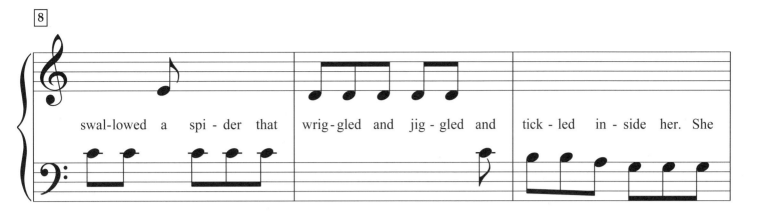

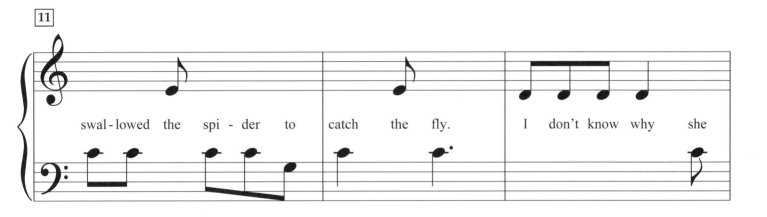

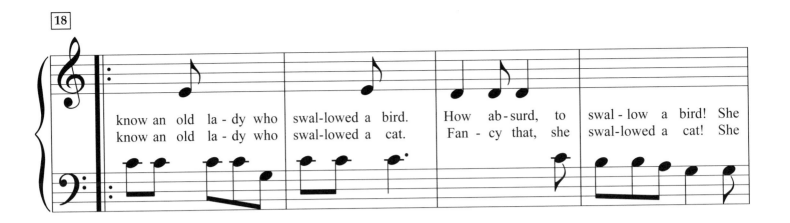

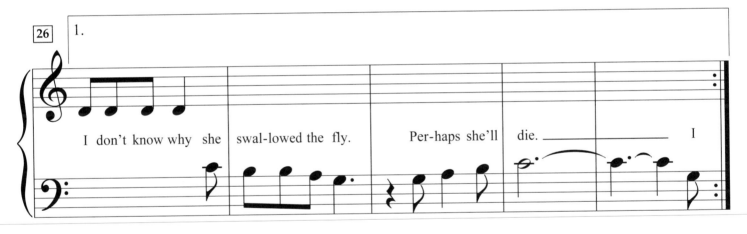

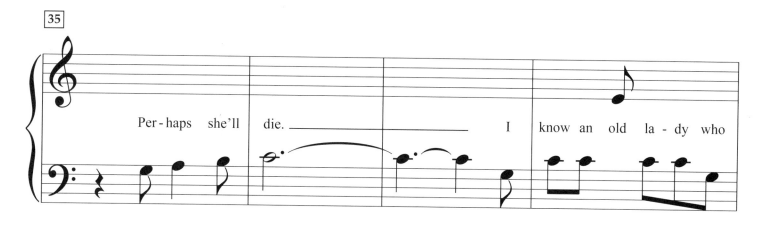

If You're Happy and You Know It

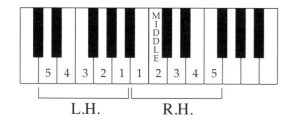

L.H.   R.H.

Words and Music by
L. Smith

Playfully

If you're hap - py and you know it, { clap your
                                      { stamp your

hands, } (clap clap) if you're hap - py and you know it, { clap your
foot, }   { stamp your

Duet Part (Student plays one octave higher than written.)

Playfully

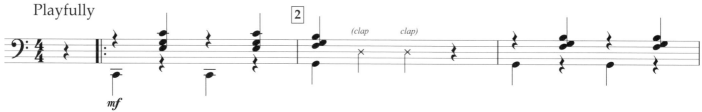

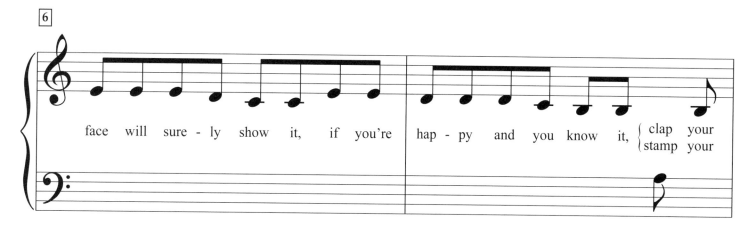

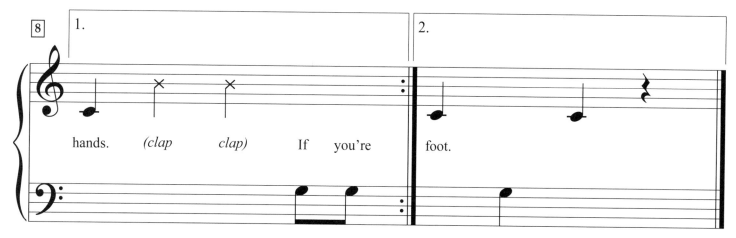

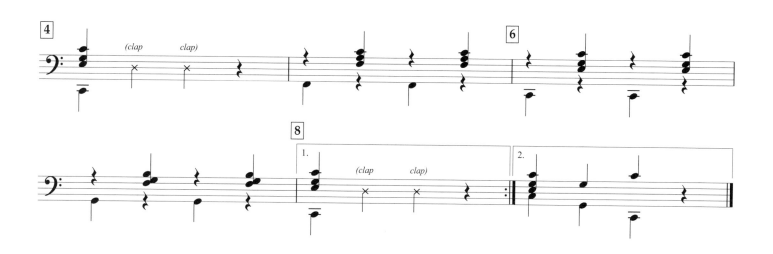

John Jacob Jingleheimer Schmidt

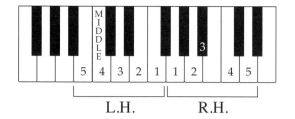

L.H.   R.H.

Traditional

Moderately fast

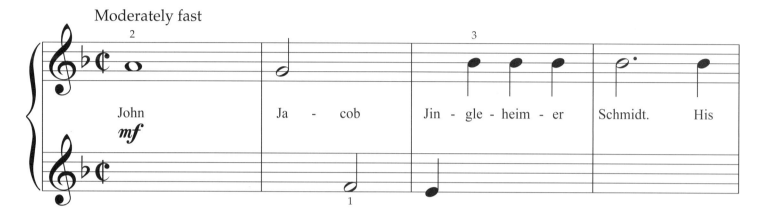

John   Ja - cob   Jin - gle - heim - er   Schmidt.   His

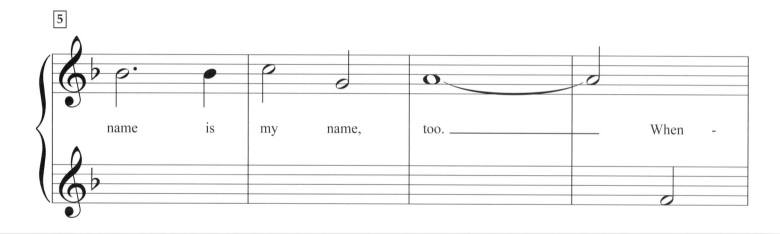

name   is   my   name,   too. _____   When -

Duet Part (Student plays one octave higher than written.)

Moderately fast

The Rhyme of the Chivalrous Shark

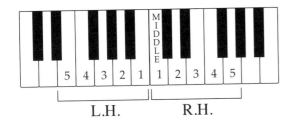

Words and Music by
Wallace Irwin

Moving along

The most | chiv - al - rous fish of the | o - cean ____ to the
read - i - ly cite you an | in - stance ____ where a
took her a - board in a | jif - fy, ____ the shark

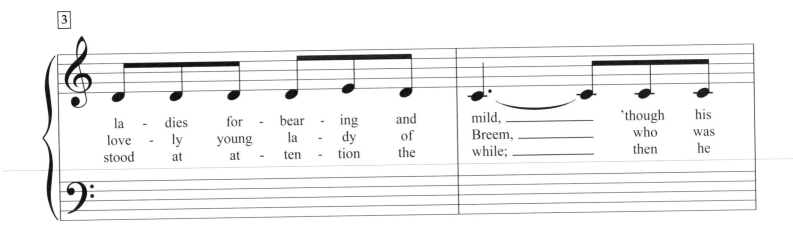

la - dies for - bear - ing and | mild, ____ 'though his
love - ly young la - dy of | Breem, ____ who was
stood at at - ten - tion the | while; ____ then he

Duet Part (Student plays one octave higher than written.)

Moving along

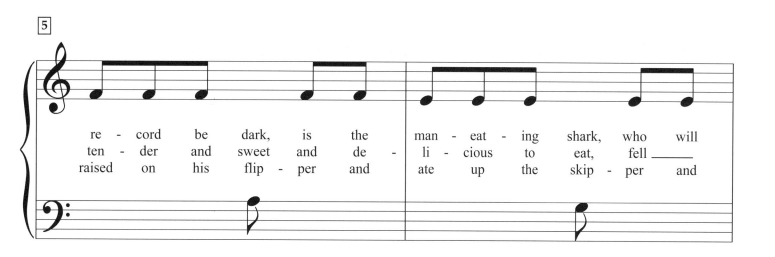

PLAYING PIANO HAS NEVER BEEN EASIER!

5-Finger Piano Collections from Hal Leonard

BEATLES! BEATLES!

8 classics, including: A Hard Day's Night • Hey Jude • Love Me Do • P.S. I Love You • Ticket to Ride • Twist and Shout • Yellow Submarine • Yesterday.
00292061..$8.99

CHILDREN'S TV FAVORITES
Themes from 8 Hit Shows

Five-finger arrangements of the themes for: Barney • Bob the Builder • Thomas the Tank Engine • Dragon Tales • PB&J Otter • SpongeBob SquarePants • Rugrats • Dora the Explorer.
00311208..$7.95

CHURCH SONGS FOR KIDS

Features five-finger arrangements of 15 sacred favorites, including: Amazing Grace • The B-I-B-L-E • Down in My Heart • Fairest Lord Jesus • Hallelu, Hallelujah! • I'm in the Lord's Army • Jesus Loves Me • Kum Ba Yah • My God Is So Great, So Strong and So Mighty • Oh, How I Love Jesus • Praise Him, All Ye Little Children • Zacchaeus • and more.
00310613..$8.99

CLASSICAL FAVORITES – 2ND EDITION

Includes 12 beloved classical pieces from Bach, Bizet, Haydn, Grieg and other great composers: Bridal Chorus • Hallelujah! • He Shall Feed His Flock • Largo • Minuet in G • Morning • Rondeau • Surprise Symphony • To a Wild Rose • Toreador Song.
00310611..$8.99

DISNEY MOVIE FUN

8 classics, including: Beauty and the Beast • When You Wish Upon a Star • Whistle While You Work • and more.
00292067..$8.99

DISNEY TUNES

Includes: Can You Feel the Love Tonight? • Chim Chim Cher-ee • Go the Distance • It's a Small World • Supercalifragilisticexpialidocious • Under the Sea • You've Got a Friend in Me • Zero to Hero.
00310375..$8.99

SELECTIONS FROM DISNEY'S PRINCESS COLLECTION VOL. 1

7 songs sung by Disney heroines – with a full-color illustration of each! Includes: Colors of the Wind • A Dream Is a Wish Your Heart Makes • I Wonder • Just Around the Riverbend • Part of Your World • Something There • A Whole New World.
00310847 ....$8.99

EENSY WEENSY SPIDER & OTHER NURSERY RHYME FAVORITES

Includes 11 rhyming tunes kids love: Hickory Dickory Dock • Humpty Dumpty • Hush, Little Baby • Jack and Jill • Little Jack Horner • Mary Had a Little Lamb • Peter, Peter Pumpkin Eater • Pop Goes the Weasel • Tom, Tom, the Piper's Son • more.
00310465..$7.95

FIRST POP SONGS

Eight timeless pop classics are presented here in accessible arrangements: Candle in the Wind • Lean on Me • Moon River • Piano Man • Tears in Heaven • Unchained Melody • What a Wonderful World • Yellow Submarine.
00123296..$8.99

FROZEN
Music from the Motion Picture

Seven popular songs from *Frozen* are featured in single-note melody lines that stay in one position in this songbook. Songs include: Do You Want to Build a Snowman? • Fixer Upper • For the First Time in Forever • In Summer • Let It Go • Love Is an Open Door • Reindeer(s) Are Better Than People. Includes lyrics and beautifully-written accompaniments.
00130374..$10.99

MODERN MOVIE FAVORITES

Eight modern movie songs including lyrics: Can't Stop the Feeling • City of Stars • Evermore • Everything Is Awesome (Awesome Remixx!!!) • How Far I'll Go • Spirit in the Sky • Try Everything • Unforgettable.
00242674..$9.99

POP HITS FOR FIVE-FINGER PIANO

8 hot hits that even beginners can play, including: Cups (When I'm Gone) • Home • I Won't Give Up • Love Story • Next to Me • Skyfall • What Makes You Beautiful • When I Was Your Man. These books also include optional duet parts for a teacher or parent to play that makes the student sound like a pro!
00123295..$9.99

THE SOUND OF MUSIC

8 big-note arrangements of popular songs from this perennial favorite musical, including: Climb Ev'ry Mountain • Do-Re-Mi • Edelweiss • The Lonely Goatherd • My Favorite Things • Sixteen Going on Seventeen • So Long, Farewell • The Sound of Music.
00310249..$10.99

SELECTIONS FROM *STAR WARS*
arr. Robert Schultz

Based on the fantastic series of *Star Wars* movies, these songs were carefully selected and arranged by Robert Schultz at the five finger level. Included in the folio are: Anakin's Theme • Augie's Great Municipal Band • Cantina Band • Duel of the Fates • The Imperial March • Luke and Leia • Princess Leia's Theme • Star Wars (Main Title) • Yoda's Theme.
00321903..$9.99

HAL•LEONARD®
www.halleonard.com